Badass B***S***

Helping Young Men Identify and
Reject Toxic Ideas About Dating,
Relationships, Women and Sex

Contents

Preface

This book is entitled, **Badass B***S***: Helping Young Men Identify and Reject Toxic Ideas About Dating, Relationships, Women and Sex.**

It is a long title, and an unusual one, so I will begin by telling you a bit about myself and then I will explain why I wrote this book.

My background is the television production industry.

I used to write, produce and direct television shows for a living, and then I transitioned into writing and publishing books.

I have written several books, including two memoirs.

One of those memoirs is entitled, **So, Why Have You Never Been Married?: A Memoir of Love, Loss and Lunacy"**.
www.sowhyhaveyouneverbeenmarried.com)

It's a very funny book – or so my readers tell me – but it's a serious book too, chronicling my real-life experiences in the world of dating and relationships over a period of several decades.

Why did I write that book?

I am a story-teller, first and foremost, and I challenged myself to recount my romantic history – the good, the bad and the ugly – in the form of a memoir, not only to preserve my memories, but to engage, amuse, entertain and inform readers - and perhaps, to even comfort others who have had similar experiences.

While not wishing to blow my own horn too much, I have had readers tell me that my memoir is one of the best books that they have ever read.

My book is not a "dating guide" or "relationship advice" book – it is a narrative – which means that it tells a story in the style of a novel – a story based on real events.

Although it is not a "how to" book, there is still a lot that people can learn by reading it.

I have been planning for some time to write a companion piece to that memoir in which I would revisit some of the situations and events that I described in it and explore the lessons that could be learned from them, both from my own behaviour and that of others.

I have wanted to write that book because I believe that my experiences have taught me some valuable lessons about dating, relationships, women and sex – lessons which I could share with others – especially young men.

I understand a lot of things *now* that I didn't when I was younger – and if I *had* understood them back then I might have spared myself and others a whole lot of pain.

However, while I have been *planning* to write *my book*, a lot of other people have already written *their books* –

thereby creating a substantial body of work in the "dating and relationships" niche, both online and offline.

In May of 2013, I received an email from another internet marketer about one of the most popular products on Clickbank.

If you are not familiar with Clickbank, it is one of the largest marketplaces for digital products on the internet.

Products on Clickbank are given what is called a "gravity rating", based upon the number of internet marketers – known as "affiliates" - who are making sales of that product in a given week.

A gravity rating of 6 or above is considered good – but the product that was being written about in the email that I received on May 8 had a gravity rating of 281.80!

With a gravity rating like that, it was likely selling *thousands* of copies per month.

And what was it?

A so-called "dating guide" for men called **The Tao of Badass** by Josh Pellicer.

I hadn't heard of **The Tao of Badass** at that time and I wanted to learn more about it.

So, I went to the official website (www.thetaoofbadass.com) and watched the promotional video for it.

Given the title, I wasn't exactly *expecting* to find common sense tips and advice that might help men – and, especially, *young* men - avoid the kinds of problems that I and millions of other men like me have experienced in their relationships with women.

That's what the book *I* was planning to write would be about.

But I wasn't prepared for what I found, either.

Remember – we are talking about one of the best-selling products in the entire Clickbank marketplace – a marketplace with tens of thousands of products!

Given its enormous popularity, I assumed that **The Tao of Badass** had to be fulfilling *some kind of need* in the marketplace – and I suppose it is – and to the *extent that it is*, we all have a serious problem, in my opinion.

As I stated - my first exposure to the **Tao of Badass** "way of thinking" about dating, relationships, women and sex - if you will - was watching the promotional video for it.

In the interests of transparency, I have not purchased the **Tao of Badass** product – nor would I encourage anyone else to do so.

But *I have* watched the promotional video for it a number of times.

That video is 47 minutes long – almost the exact length of the television documentaries that I used to produce on serious subjects like missing children, wife assault and heart disease.

You can pack a lot of really valuable information into 47 minutes of screen time.

Or, you can present the kind of "ideas and attitudes" – that you find in the promotional video for **The Tao of Badass** – which I would not wish to dignify with the term "information".

Now – I wish to be clear here – I do not know, for sure, what **The Tao of Badass** was intended to be.

I do not know whether it was intended as a joke, a satire, a clever but cynical, "con job" designed to prey upon men who are young, naïve, impressionable and weak – or whether the creator of the product *actually believes* what he is saying.

What I do know is this – there is a video which, as of the time of this writing, is posted on a website whose main keyword, "the tao of badass", is being searched over 27,000 times a month - and the product that it is promoting is one of the best-selling products in the entire Clickbank marketplace.

So – *however* it was intended – the fact is that the ideas and attitudes about dating, relationships, women and sex that are presented in the video *are being consumed* by a lot of people – mostly young men, presumably.

Ideas and attitudes which are – *in my opinion* – not

only toxic and sinister, but which, if taken seriously, have a better chance of resulting in a meeting with a prison warden than they do of helping to attract women.

To be honest, I cannot believe that *anyone* could take these ideas seriously - or that anyone would spend money on a product that espouses them – but we are living in a culture in which *anything* is possible.

When a man in Ohio can kidnap three young women and keep them chained up in his basement *for a decade* while he repeatedly sexually abuses them – you know that you are living in a culture in which *anything* is possible.

Once again – it may well be that **The Tao of Badass** is a *great big joke* that everyone is in on but *me*.

That would not be surprising since I'm not exactly "in the loop" when it comes to knowing just how impressionable and naïve adolescent males are these days, although it seems that it was only yesterday that I was the age of the people who are now reading **The Tao of Badass**.

But even if it *is* a joke – it is in *extremely* bad taste.

And, even if it *was* intended as a joke or a satire, there may *still* be people consuming it who do not *recognize* it is a joke or a satire – and those people could be influenced by it and could hurt others – in my opinion.

To be fair, **The Tao of Badass** is not the only

product out there that espouses a "badass" approach to women – and to dating, sex and relationships, too.

It might be fair to say that there is something of a "badass" movement, of which **The Tao of Badass** is merely representative, and that the fundamental principle upon which that movement was founded is that being a "badass" is good.

Hence, this book.

My purpose here is to examine the ideas and attitudes presented in the promotional video for the **Tao of Badass** product – ideas and attitudes which , as I have said, I believe are *representative* of the "badass philosophy", if you will - and to expose them for what they are – toxic, sinister, infantile and dangerous.

It is my hope that this report will help men – especially *young men* – identify these kinds of ideas and attitudes and reject them.

Why?

Because being a badass is *bullshit*.

You will get a whole lot further in life – and enjoy a lot more success with women – by simply being a good guy.

No woman – especially not *the kind of woman* that you would want to spend any time with – wants to be with a badass.

Why would she?

What do you get out of hanging around with a badass – other than abuse?

And one last note about the tone of this book.

You may have noticed that I am talking to you like an adult because that is what I want to help you become.

I could have adopted a tone that is more closely aligned with that of the subject matter that is being examined – I.e., I could have written a book that sounds like **The Tao of Badass**, but that would not have helped you to leave the world of adolescent thinking and behaviour behind as the adult tone I am using now.

There is no advantage in life to thinking and acting like a kid – much less, a "badass" jerk.

The great pleasures of life are really reserved for adults – it's a grown-up world, and the sooner you take your rightful place in it, the sooner you will enjoy all the wonderful things that life has to offer.

CHAPTER 1

The Bait

I stated in the Preface to this book that I used to write and produce broadcast television programs and series.

Prior to that, I taught English and Film at the high school and university levels.

As an undergraduate and as a graduate student of English Literature, I analyzed a great many literary works to discover what they were trying to say and how they were trying to say it.

In this book, I am going to undertake the very same type of critical analysis of the text of the promotional video for **The Tao of Badass.**

In doing so, I am not suggesting that it is, in any way, a *literary* work - but it is a substantial piece of work, nonetheless, containing thoughts, ideas and attitudes that have the power to influence – especially if *thousands* - if not *tens of thousands* of men - are being exposed to them.

For the purpose of this book, I had the *narration track* of the video – that is, the words that we hear the narrator say - transcribed, and I will be quoting from that document extensively.

The video has a visual component, as well, of course, which we will not be examining in this book. The visuals consist of a "hand-drawing" animation for about the first half of the video and a series of slides in the second half.

As a former television and video producer, I have an appreciation of good production values, and I should say that the video is well-produced and that the visual elements effectively support the text.

Having said that, I believe that the *fundamental message* of the **Tao of Badass** video can be ascertained by focusing exclusively on the text.

I have broken the text of the video into six sections, each of which will be examined in a separate chapter.

And so, let's begin:

Prior to the start of the video, there is a warning to viewers that reads:

The following presentation is controversial and may be offensive to some audiences. Viewer discretion is advised.

This warning is significant, in my view, in that it acknowledges that the content of the video could well offend some viewers.

Let's now examine the first section of the narration track:

Hi. My name is Josh and this is a fish. In just a few minutes, I'm going to show you how this fish will help you get laid and I will do it without

**teaching you cheesy pick-up lines that don't
work, without letting you spend a dime on
dinners and drinks and without anyone ever
noticing you're using this technique on them.**

**But first, I've got to warn you - I've taught this
technique you're about to learn to over 110,000
guys just like you who live in over 30 countries
around the world and it's going to make hot
women stare at you and uncontrollably chase
you. But to be fair to the other 100,000-plus guys
who've shoved money in my pocket to teach
them this technique already, I'm only going to be
able to leave this video up for 24 hours. So this is,
literally, the only chance you will get to see this
video all the way through and if you actually
think you have something better to do than learn
this technique, then you're either gay – not that
there's anything wrong with that if you are – or
so old, you piss dust.**

After introducing himself as "Josh" in the first line of
the text, Pellicer refers to a graphic of a "fish" which
appears on the screen, and states that this fish is
going to help *you* – the viewer – "get laid".

Not only that – the fish is going to help you achieve
that goal without you having to resort to using any
"cheesy pick-up lines that don't work", or even
having to "spend a dime on dinners and drinks".

 Plus, *no one will even notice* that you are using a
technique on them.

So, what he have, within the first few seconds of the video, is the *bait* - the promise of a *technique* designed to help you have sex with women which:

1. Doesn't require cheesy pick-up lines

2. Won't cost you anything

3. No one will notice you are even using on them

We now see how appropriate the image of the fish in the first line of text is - *you* are the fish - and the bait being dangled in front of you is a technique for meeting women and having sex with them which is easy, free and undetectable.

The text is certainly not subtle – in fact, quite the opposite. It seems to have been written with a sledgehammer, not a keyboard. The use of the term "get laid" is deliberate – a vulgar expression that men of all ages are probably familiar with – and while some men – myself included – may find the term offensive, there is no uncertainty as to what the product that is being promoted here is promising to deliver to you – *sex*.

So, we shall not refer to this as a "dating guide" and recognize it for what it is - a guide to seducing women.

In the second paragraph, a key theme is introduced – the need for you to take *immediate action* and gobble up the bait. Why? Because "over 110,000 guys just like you who live in over 30 countries around the world" already have – and to be fair to them, Pellicer says, he is "only going to be able to leave this video up for 24 hours".

As we saw in the first paragraph - and as we shall see throughout the video - Pellicer is not reluctant to hit you over the head to get you to give him $67 for his secret system for seducing women, and in Paragraph 2 he reveals that he is also willing to resort to a blatant lie.

I first viewed the video on May 8, and as of June 6 - almost a month later - it was still available on the website. Yet, Pellicer states that the video will only be up for 24 hours.

He also makes another revealing claim for the product in Paragraph 2, saying that "it's going to make hot women stare at you and uncontrollably chase you".

The use of the word "uncontrollably" is noteworthy, as the theme of *controlling women* is another major one in the video.

In the last sentence of Paragraph 2, one of the key marketing strategies of the video – defining the target market - is introduced, with the goal, of course, of catching as many fish as possible.

Just in case you were about to reject his secret method to "get women to *uncontrollably* chase you" and were about to bail on the video – Pellicer attempts to draw you back in by arguing that there are really only two types of guys who might actually have something better to do than to watch the video – gay guys and guys so old they "piss dust".

Unless you're in one of those categories – or, perhaps, both – you better stay put.

Let's move on to Paragraph 3, in which he continues to explicitly define his target market:

If you consider yourself an above average or even typical guy, stick around. This is totally for you and if you watch until the end of the webinar, I'm going to give you the system that is literally step-by -step and is proven to create sexual intrigue that is so compelling and so powerful that almost any girl you use it on will find their panties around their knees soaked to the max before she can even say, "My name is …"

In this section, Pellicer continues to define his market, which now includes "above average" and "typical" guys. Up to now, he's only been prepared to give up on gay and old men. In this paragraph, he's seems to be letting guys who are below average off the hook.

Everyone else should "stick around" because what he has to offer is "totally for you." And to make sure you *do* hang in "until the end of the webinar", he raises the stakes even higher. What he is offering is now no longer a "technique" but a "system – one which is "so compelling and so powerful" that "almost any girl you use it on will find their panties around their knees soaked to the max before she can even say, 'My name is....'"

Remember the theme of "controlling women" that we spoke about a moment ago?

Here it is again.

However, now, the women have gone from simply chasing you around *uncontrollably* to finding their panties – soaked *to the max, yet!* – around their knees.

How, exactly, did their panties get *there*?

Who knows? The girls just *found them there*.

They must be under some kind of spell.

In the following paragraph, the theme of controlling women against their will is stated even more explicitly:

Listen, I pulled this off so many times, I've lost count. It even works if she thinks you're unattractive. In fact, if you follow my step-by-step method to the letter, it's literally out of her control. She has to respond. Wouldn't that be a secret you would love to know? Well, this is the fact. All women go through the same exact process every time they decide to sleep with a guy and trust me, you've never seen anything like this before. So make sure you watch this video to the very end.

What we're presented with is a "step-by-step method" to get a woman to respond in a way that is "literally out of her control".

No wonder it "even works if she thinks you're unattractive".

Why wouldn't it, if her response is "literally out of her control"?

So far, Pellicer hasn't told us very much about what the method *actually is* – but he has promised to – as long as we "watch this video to the very end".

However, before he gets around to revealing his secret method, he wants to tell us a story.

What kind of story?

A "sex story".

First, I'm going to tell you a sex story. Yeah, I know. Most guys will tell you all about the different media appearances they've done, all the books they've authored, blah, blah. And yeah, I could bore you with that crap. I have a credentialed resume that would make the biggest player you know run home to his momma.

Listen, if you're smart, you don't give a damn about that and I bet you don't. You probably just want the juice, the secret sauce, and I'm going to get to that in just a few seconds right after my sex story.

Deal?

Cool.

So how does a skinny, little, loser-looking dude go from zero to sleeping with up to 15 new "hotties" a month? Did I get rich? Did I memorize line after lame-ass line? Did I put on pheromone cologne?

Hell, no.

If I were to accept Pellicer's word for it - which I *wouldn't* - I have made a cardinal mistake in the Preface of this report by talking about the books *I've* authored.

Good thing I didn't bring up the four university degrees I have.

Not like our humble narrator – although he just *happens* to have dropped the fact that he has "a credentialed resume that would make the biggest player you know run home to his momma".

Really? I wonder what those credentials might be.

He doesn't say, and doesn't feel the need to – because "if you're smart, you don't give a damn about that."

All *you're* interested in knowing is how a "skinny, little, loser-looking dude" like him went "from zero to sleeping with up to 15 new 'hotties' a month".

Note that he introduces another of the *central themes* of the video here – that just about any guy in the world – with the exception of those who are gay or "pissing dust", perhaps – can have sex with the most attractive women on the planet *without doing anything* – anything other than giving him 67 bucks for his secret system, that is.

That's "the juice, the secret sauce" that *you* are interested in – and it's also the *bait* that he's been dangling in front of your nose all along and which he will continue to dangle all the way to the end of the video because that is what he is selling.

This video has one objective – to get you to *buy* a series of tricks and techniques that purports to teach you how to have sex with virtually every attractive woman who crosses your path – but that is not surprising, as it is a *sales video*.

He wants you to *buy the juice* – but he says he's going to give it to you – or, at least, *some* of it.

After he tells his sex story, that is.

CHAPTER 2

An Epiphany

Let's quickly recap what we have learned so far.

We have learned that Pellicer has a technique, system or method that he has *already* shared with over 110,000 guys in over 30 countries around the world that is *so powerful* that it makes women completely lose control and have sex with anybody who knows how to use it – even guys that they find unattractive.

They will even have sex with "skinny, little, loser-looking" dudes like the author himself.

So far, he hasn't said *what* it is, or how *he* happened to learn or discover it.

But he's *going to* – he's going to spill all the beans right here in this video – after he tells his "sex story" - and alienates the leper community at the same time.

The truth is pretty brutal. I was an absolute leper with women until I discovered the system. If you look up "whipped" in the dictionary, it would say, "See Josh Pellicer here." In fact, if I hadn't hit complete rock bottom, I would probably still be terrible to this day. You see, several years ago, I was living with my complete Ice Queen of an ex-girlfriend in North Carolina. She was hot, young and she knew it. You know - a "total Barbie" who always gets what she wants - and I thought she was amazing in bed.

Now that I've been with a few hundred more women, I wouldn't even rate her a "5". Listen, back then, the old Josh did anything she wanted. She wanted to move to North Carolina. I said, "Okay, let's go." She wanted to keep in touch with her ex-boyfriend. I told her, "It's okay, I understand."

She wanted me to pay for the apartment. I don't want to look like a deadbeat so I said, "I will work two jobs, no problem." I just wanted to make her happy. But one brutally hot day, I come home from a 14-hour shift at the coffee shop I worked at to find her freaking out. She told me that her dad was making a surprise visit and she never told him that she was dating anyone and definitely not that she was living with someone and the worst part - he was showing up that night.

So she told me to get all my stuff and leave the house for a couple of days so he wouldn't find out that I lived there with her, and, like the little boy that I was, I left.

I got all my stuff, packed it into my little crappy, black Honda Accord and drove out, not having any idea where I would go. I didn't have any friends in town and I was way too proud to ask some random person if I could stay with them. So I drove around until I found a vacant house that was for sale and I parked behind it, hoping no one would notice me sleeping in my car. It wouldn't have been too bad, really, but I had to do it for three days in a row and on the third day, something happened and I snapped.

See, I had to sleep with my windows open because it was way too hot to close them. But the mosquitoes were so bad that I had to use a blanket to keep them off me. So I only slept about two hours each night and I couldn't even lean the driver's seat back because all my stuff was packed in the back seat behind me. So I had to sleep sitting up in the driver's seat, covered in a blanket in the sweltering heat behind a vacant house like a hobo. And then it happened. I was half asleep and I hear, "Freeze! Put your hands where I can see them!"

I freak out, of course. So in a daze, I put my hands out the window and a swarm of police officers jogged over to my car with their guns out and aimed at my window. Apparently, the neighbor had seen a strange car parked behind the vacant lot and called the police. I guess I would have done the same thing.

After they calmed down and realized I wasn't some national threat, they asked me what I was doing there and that's when I did it. I told them that my girlfriend's dad was in town and he didn't know we were dating so I had to sleep in my car for a few days. That's when one cop turned off his flashlight, looked at the other cop in complete disbelief and turned to me and said, "Seriously?"

I was tired and I didn't have the energy to explain more so I just said, "Yeah." I think he was still trying to be professional so he told me that I needed to go somewhere else and he told me to try sleeping in the Walmart parking lot.

As he was turning to walk back to his car, I heard him say, "Poor bastard." The rest of the night, I did some serious thinking. I sort of had to because I couldn't go to sleep. Have you ever been so tired that you can't fall asleep? Well, that was me. I just sort of woke up and realized that I was a complete and utter "wuss". I was a sorry excuse for a man. If my dad knew how much of a "wuss" I had become, he would be disappointed.

So that night, I wrote a note to myself on a piece of notebook paper that said, "I will get this attraction thing handled or I will die trying." I still carry that note around with me to this day.

So I grabbed the first thing I knew to look at out of my backseat – my psychology notebook from when I went to college in Florida. I opened it randomly and I started reading and I didn't know if I was delirious from no sleep for three days or if something just snapped and my IQ jumped 50 points. But I suddenly noticed a theory that my professor taught me that just went in one ear and out the other – "propinquity" – a $10, word which is probably why I never remembered it in the first place.

So I read all my notes on this "propinquity" thing

and I thought, "Well, screw it. What the hell do I have to lose? I will try it out tomorrow." So the next morning, after rinsing off with paper towels in the bathroom at a place called **Panera Bread**, seriously, I went into work and I started using it on the customers.

The first time I used it, nothing. The second time, nothing again. But the third time, she smiled, asked me my name and said she would like to hang out after I got off work. I thought, "Holy crap! It actually worked."

So that night I hung out with her for an hour or two. No, nothing happened with her because I still didn't know what the hell I was doing. Plus, I wasn't single yet.

Then afterwards, I went back, broke up with my girlfriend. My car was already packed with my crap anyway and I spent the whole night looking through my notes to find other techniques I could try out. I did that every day for a week, then two weeks, then a month, then six months.

A year went by and I had read 5 psychology text books, 12 dating advice books, 2 etiquette books and watched over 400 hours of training videos on building rapport, subliminal messaging, seduction, attraction, body language, personality typing. I was a machine and eventually I began to see patterns, things that allowed me to plug myself into an attraction switchboard.

From then on, arousing, attracting and seducing beautiful women was a piece of delicious cake to me, almost second nature. So I created brand new techniques and tricks that the world had never seen before and all to help me take advantage of those powerful patterns that I discovered.

But what were some of those techniques that I used and that thousands of guys eventually started using to get women to uncontrollably flirt, make out and sleep with me time and time again? The ones I found that worked just about 100 percent of the time on just about any kind of woman, regardless of her age, hair color, height or how "smoking hot" she was?

Well, I would like to teach some of them to you now if that's all right with you. You might want to get a pen and a piece of paper ready for this part especially since this video gets taken down in 24 hours.

I have quoted the so-called "sex story" in its entirety.

In my opinion, it is more of an "epiphany" than a "sex story" as it describes the moment of deep insight at which Pellicer realized that he had hit "complete rock bottom" and needed to make a profound change in his life.

And what was *that moment?*

When a police officer, having found him sleeping in his car in a vacant lot – while sitting upright in the front seat because all of his personal belongings were packed into the back seat – covered with a blanket to keep the mosquitoes off him in sweltering heat and said – "Poor bastard."

Remember – this is one of the *best-selling products in the entire Clickbank marketplace* – and it serves up a lame story like this!

Is there a single line – or even a single *word* – in this entire story that rings true *to you*?

Not to me, there isn't.

However, the key issue here is not *truth* – we know this guy has been lying through his teeth since he said, "Hi. My name is Josh".

Of far greater importance is the *message* expressed in the text – however far removed it may be from reality.

Because, as I have said, ideas have power – especially ideas that are being read by thousands - or tens of thousands of people - every month.

So, let's examine the "world view", if you will, of the "sex story" in greater detail.

We already know that the narrator is a "skinny little loser-looking dude" - now we find out that he's working 14 hours a day at a coffee shop.

Despite the fact that he's unattractive, he has managed to get a girlfriend – one who is "hot" and "young".

How, exactly, did that happen?

She's not just "hot" – she's a "total Barbie" – and Pellicer even thinks she's "amazing in bed" - although his opinion on that matter will change after he's "been with a few hundred more women" over the next year or two.

And what does Pellicer – the "pre-epiphany-Pellicer", that is - have to offer *her* anyway?

A skinny, little loser-looking dude with a minimum wage job?

Not much.

Yet, he seems to have a sense of *entitlement*.

He seems to think that his romantic life should be a whole lot better – rather than thanking his lucky stars that he's not sleeping alone in his car *every* night.

Nonetheless, things seem to be going along *reasonably* well with the "Ice Queen" girlfriend until – an unexpected visit from her father.

This is the incident that precipitates the entire series of events that culminates in his life-altering epiphany in the front seat of his crappy little black Honda with a blanket over his head in the middle of a heat wave.

And just what happens in that fateful incident?

His girlfriend asks him to leave the apartment for a

few days to avoid an awkward confrontation with her father whom she hasn't told that she is living with someone.

I will concede that that is not *terribly* considerate on behalf of his girlfriend – especially since Pellicer doesn't have any friends or family members to stay with – but who knows what issues *she* has with her father?

Maybe he was abusive to her or to her mother – or both.

Perhaps he has deep moral beliefs that would conflict with his daughter's lifestyle decisions.

We don't know because Pellicer doesn't tell her side of the story.

He's so self-absorbed that he probably doesn't know or even *care to know* very much about his girlfriend's past.

His only concern is how "hot" she is.

But, is the fact that he's too much of a "wuss" to stand up to her or to confront her father with the truth about their living arrangement *her* fault?

And what does the fact that he is a "sorry excuse for man" have to do with the issue of "attraction"?

It's bad enough, in my view, that his "sex story" is a gigantic crock – couldn't it, at least, make logical sense?

Apparently, not.

One of the best-selling products in the Clickbank marketplace, and it doesn't have the logic of squirrel poop.

But, back to our story - Pellicer spends three nights in a row sleeping in his car until a cop savagely cuts him to the quick by calling him a "poor bastard".

And that's it.

He snaps.

Digs out an old psychology textbook from the back of his car and comes up the word "propinquity".

Yes, "propinquity".

And then, what does he do?

After rinsing himself off in the men's room of Panera Bread – an especially pathetic image - he gives his new "propinquity" technique a shot.

Just like that.

Starts using it on the customers at the coffee shop – in violation of company policy, one would imagine – but it doesn't work anyway.

Not the first time, that is - but by the third time – Bingo! – the unsuspecting victim of his "propinquity" technique tells Pellicer that "she would like to hang out after work".

And, from then on, there is no looking back for him.

He immediately breaks up with his girlfriend and spends *the next year* reading "5 psychology text books, 12 dating advice books [and] 2 etiquette books" and watching "over 400 hours of training videos on building rapport, subliminal messaging, seduction, attraction, body language, [and] personality typing."

"Eventually," he says, he begins to "see patterns, things that [allow him] to plug [himself] into an attraction switchboard." Once that happens, "arousing, attracting and seducing beautiful women [is] a piece of delicious cake to [him], almost second nature."

He becomes a veritable machine, cranking out "brand new techniques and tricks that the world had never seen before" – techniques to get women to "uncontrollably flirt, make out and sleep with [him] time and time again."

And *now* he wants to teach these techniques and tricks *to you* – not just the "propinquity" technique –but all of the other ones that he has spent the past few years inventing, too.

And, once again, he reminds you that *you had better act fast because* "this video gets taken down in 24 hours".

What's one more blatant lie after a whopper of a tale like that?

And what if you *don't* act now?

What if you just walk away from this video *right now* and go your merry way, armed with the "propinquity" technique?

You didn't have *that one* at the start of the video, did you?

So, you're already *way ahead* of the game.

Just in case you *are* thinking these thoughts, too, Pellicer warns you that *if you do bail now* you will be leaving a very valuable technique on the table.

Remember, these techniques will get you results instantly but I'm just barely scratching the surface here and pay close attention to the last technique I teach you because that's where I'm going to reveal the number one simple "bizarro chick trick" that you've never heard of before, that got me 90 percent of my success with women right away and how thinking like this fish is going to make you better with women than anyone you've ever known.

Okay – better lose that thought of bailing on *this* video.

If you do, you'll miss out on the "bizarro chick trick" that Pellicer is about to reveal.

The one that is responsible for 90% of his success – the one which "you've never heard of before" and which is going to make you "better with women than anyone you've ever known".

Wouldn't want to miss out on that, would you?

Especially since only about 110,000 other guys in the world are already in on it.

So, what are we to make of Pellicer's "sex story"?

It's obviously a pile of horse manure, but what does it mean?

What is the *significance* of it?

Simple.

To demonstrate that Pellicer couldn't be transformed into God's Gift to Women until he stopped being a "wuss".

That is, until he became a "badass" – although he hasn't introduced the term to us yet.

He had to stop doing nice things for his girlfriend - like working 14 hours a day to pay the rent, agreeing to move to North Carolina and allowing her to keep in touch with her ex-boyfriend – before he could be radically transformed into a sex machine.

He had to hit "complete rock bottom" - sleeping upright in the front seat of his car - before he could work up the nerve to break up with his girlfriend and start digging through dusty old college psychology textbooks in search of tricks and techniques that would allow him to have sex with "up to 15 new 'hotties' a month".

While he was still broke and living in his car!

One can, apparently, only pull off that kind *of radical transformation* by having a tough guy, authority figure tell you what a "poor bastard" you are.

And the *really important thing* is that, having survived his own "dark night of the soul", as it were, he wants to *teach you* some of the techniques for attracting and bedding women that he has devised – "if that's alright with you".

At least he's not keeping all of these precious techniques to himself.

Nope - he's teaching it to guys all over the world – to over 110,000 guys from over 30 countries – guys just like you!

And now he wants to teach *you* – if that's *alright* with you.

But before you hand over your hard-earned cash, he's going to let you in on a few more of his secret tricks and techniques – well, perhaps they're not *all that secret* since, as we pointed out a moment ago, over 100,000 guys from over 30 countries *already* know them.

 And you have to wonder - if they're really *that* effective (15 "hotties" a month is a lot of "hotties" for *anyone*) - aren't some of the 110,000 guys already sharing them on Twitter or Facebook – or with their personal friends?

CHAPTER 3

Tricks and Techniques

In the previous chapter, we learned all about Pellicer's epiphany of self-discovery.

The one that compelled him to break up with his girlfriend and spend every waking hour studying the patterns of human attraction until he came up with dozens - or, perhaps, even hundreds - of ways to attract and have sex with women.

"Propinquity" was only the first of the compelling and powerful tricks and techniques that he came up with during his *annus mirabilis* of scientific discovery and invention.

Although he doesn't say so *explicitly*, we have to assume that he was forced to cut back on his hours at the coffee shop or, perhaps, quit his job *entirely*, since devising strategies "that work just about 100 percent of the time on just about any kind of woman regardless of her age, hair color, height or how smoking hot she [is]" requires a lot of time and energy.

It's hard to schedule that kind of demanding research work around 14-hour shifts at the coffee shop, no matter how highly motivated you may be.

Plus, as mentioned, he was sleeping with the 15 new "hotties" a month – another significant drain on his time and energy.

In the next section of the text, he lets us in on a few of the tricks and techniques that he came up with:

The first technique has to do with the chick's mouth. I know - chick's mouth - you want to put something in it. I get that, but before you run off and do that, let me tell you the secret. Did you know that if you look at a woman's mouth while she's talking to you, that you will subconsciously make her think about sleeping with you?

This is called a "sexual trigger". Sexual triggers are secret techniques that bypass all of her barriers and turn her on without her knowledge. Using sexual triggers is like using inception to make her want to sleep with you. They are the cornerstone of unrivaled success with women and I'm going to reveal where you can get dozens of these near the end of this video. These triggers are so stealth that they actually bypass a woman's logical brain – and yes, she has one – and they speak directly to her emotional brain. And let me tell you, her emotional brain is this damn big. Every woman's is.

Here's another sexual trigger. Did you know that over 90 percent of guys turn women off before they even open their mouths by facing them directly with their bodies? Yeah, I didn't know that either. Turning your chest toward a girl too early is a subconscious sign of neediness and it completely destroys sexual attraction.

Well how about this little trick? Before you really

start talking about something serious with a girl, try saying this. "I get a sense that you're open to trying new things and that makes me feel comfortable and at ease."

Then continue the conversation with her. Doing this at the right time will subconsciously compel her to chase you. It uses a psychological trick called "consistency" and it's a biological shortcut that skips over all her red flags and plugs you directly into her love center. I don't think I need to warn you not to use that one irresponsibly.

Impressive stuff.

The first of the tricks and techniques revealed in this section of text has to do with a woman's mouth.

"Did you know", Pellicer asks, "that if you look at a woman's mouth while she's talking to you, that you will subconsciously make her think about sleeping with you?"

Note the use of the word, "subconsciously". The woman is thinking about sleeping with you "subconsciously".

How would he know that?

Because it's a "sexual trigger" – and a "sexual trigger" is able to "bypass all her barriers and turn her on without her knowledge".

"Subconsciously….without her knowledge"….these words are not chosen by accident.

And how is this technique able to do that?

Because it is a "stealth" technique.

As for the second secret trigger that Pellicer reveals in this section, he begins by asking, "Did you know that over 90 percent of guys turn women off before they even open their mouths by facing them directly with their bodies?"

This, Pellicer explains, "is a subconscious sign of neediness and it completely destroys sexual attraction".

Once again, no explanation as to the process of verifying these scientific discoveries.

The third of the three "tricks" revealed in this section of text consists of saying, "I get a sense that you're open to trying new things and that makes me feel comfortable and at ease" at the precise moment in a conversation with a women before you begin "talking about something serious".

This technique "uses a psychological trick called "consistency", Pellicer explains, and it's a "biological shortcut that skips over all of her red flags and plugs you directly into her love center."

He must have felt some trepidation in revealing that last weapon of psychological seduction as he is compelled to add, "I don't think I need to warn you not to use that one irresponsibly."

To sum up this section of the text, we now have four

of Pellicer's most effective tricks and techniques for achieving "unrivaled success with women". They are:

- Propinquity

- Looking at a women's mouth while she is speaking

- Not turning your chest towards a girl too early in a conversation

- Consistency

Quite a potent arsenal, wouldn't you agree?

Hard to imagine that there could be *anything* left in his bag of tricks - but wait! - this is just the tip of the iceberg!

He has lots more to reveal, including a whole bunch of lies which, "*if you don't see for yourself*", are going to prevent you from ever succeeding with the "super hot" chicks – that is, the "9's and 10's".

Look, I know this all sounds ridiculously simple. Well, it is ridiculously simple but I've got a lot more to share with you if you really want to get the 9's and 10's. These figures are going to get you in the front door but they're not going to get you all the way home.

So let me teach you exactly how to get all the way home. But first, I need to reveal a big, big lie to you because if you don't see these lies for yourself, you will always be invisible to the

"super hot" chicks. I'm going to start by telling you what women don't want because you've been lied to.

The big news in the above paragraph is that *you've* been lied to - by *someone other than the narrator of this video.*

In the next section of the text, Pellicer will explain what those lies are and who's been telling them to you.

CHAPTER 4

What Women Really Want

The next section of text is, perhaps, the most ironic of the entire video because in it, Pellicer exposes the lies promulgated by a "certain group of people" regarding what women really want.

The irony derives from the fact that Pellicer has been lying from the moment we met him about the video being taken down within the next 24 hours, but he is either unaware of the irony or unfazed by it.

 Perhaps, when it comes to liars, he is applying the "it takes one to know one" theory.

Let's examine the actual text in which he exposes the so-called lies:

A certain group of people want you to believe that women want this crap but they don't want it. So let's start from the top. Money. You think women want money? Well, guess what. You've been lied to about money and I'm pissed off about it. And guess what else. Women are not attracted to big muscles. Most women are actually repulsed by guys who look all "steroided up". And it's not a full head of hair.

In 2007, a survey revealed that ninety-seven percent of women actually find bald men sexy. Ninety-seven percent! And it's not good looks either. I remember seeing an interview with Brad

Pitt where he admitted that he could not get a date when he first moved to Hollywood. Brad Pitt!

Recall that earlier in the video, Pellicer was careful to define the market for his **Tao of Badass** product as including *everyone other than* 1) gay men, 2) old men who "piss dust" and 3) guys who are below average – a rather inclusive audience - for the simple reason that he wants to sell as many copies of his product as possible.

In the section of text cited above, he is calling out specific groups of men whom he fears might *self-disqualify* because of a belief that no matter what they do, they aren't going to achieve success with women anyway – men who lack money, big muscles or a full head of hair.

And what is the fastest and easiest way to overcome these "buyer obstacles"?

Simply *ignore* the evidence to the contrary provided by the George Clooneys, Brad Pitts and Tom Bradys of the world - and assert that people who tell you that women are attracted to guys with money, muscles and hair are liars.

Not only have *you* been lied to, but *Pellicer* is "pissed off about it".

If *you're* the one who has been lied to, why is *he* pissed off about it?

Because he's trying to sell you a $67 product that will

"get you all the way home" with "super hot" women and he doesn't want *you* to let the fact that you don't have money, muscles or a full head of hair stand in the way of that sale.

So, he tells you that it's all a big lie. Women don't want any of *that* stuff.

Nope – they want something else.

They want "pre-selection".

Now let me tell you what it's actually all about. It's all about something called pre-selection. That's making her think that other women already want you. Let me tell you how that works. Women have what's called a "filter mechanism". That basically means that it's her job to filter out weak and undesired men and you have what's called an "approach mechanism". That's the thing that makes you kick yourself and feel like a "wuss" if you don't go and talk to a girl you're attracted to.

These two things do not mix. They're like oil and water and if you walk up to a woman with your normal approach mechanism like ninety-nine percent of guys do, then she's going to filter you right out. Just like oil and water. This is a fact and it has been hardwired into the females of our species and just about every other species on the planet too, including the fish. Check this out. When most female fish look for a mate, they search for a male who's the brightest color.

That's because if a male is a brighter color, it means he's healthier and they look for those healthy genes to help their offspring survive. But when two males are close to the same brightness, something very strange happens. The females all mate with the one male that the other females are mating with. It's just how they are wired and women are the exact same way.

That's right. We're all thinking like fish, but if you're going to be a fish, I want you to be a piranha. So here's a question you might want to know the answer to. How do women know that other women are attracted to you just by looking at you? Well, here's the beautiful thing. They don't. They're absolutely guessing and they're pretty good at it too. But they're not perfect at it.

If you know the exact techniques, the exact recipe for sex that I'm going to reveal to you in just a second, you can make any woman think that other women are climbing over each other to get at your jock.

Just by mimicking the right thing, all women around you will begin to fall for it one by one regardless of what you look like, how much money you have or how good you actually are with women. But if you thought it was money, success or fame that women were attracted to, guess what. You're not alone. So did I, man, and it's because this "pre-selection" thing is the most well-guarded secret in the world. But do you know who's guarding it? The media and, more

specifically, the magazines.

Let's face it – it's not easy to make a lot of money, to develop big muscles or to grow hair if you don't have any – so if women *really are* attracted to men who have some or all of those attributes, a lot of other guys are going to be SOL.

Pellicer knows that, of course, so he tells you that it's all a pack of lies.

If what women really want is "pre-selection" – that changes everything, doesn't it?

"Pre-selection" is not something that you *actually have* – it's something you can *fake*.

"If you know the exact techniques", Pellicer claims – "the exact recipe for sex" - then presto! – "you can make any woman think that other women are climbing over each other to get at your jock".

He wants you to believe that all you really need to do to attract women is employ his "exact recipe for sex" and mimic "the right thing".

That will make women "think" that other women are fighting over you - fighting over "your jock", that is – presumably, *while you are still wearing it*.

In other words – just *use deception*.

And Pellicer is here to say that *any guy* can do that.

Any guy who forks over $67, that is.

In the next section of text, he takes the rhetoric to an even high level:

Try this. Just pick up a chick's magazine and try to read it. It's chockfull of nonsense that they're saying men want. If chick magazines told the truth about what guys wanted, they would all say this: Step one; be hotter. Step two; give great head.

Just like women obsess over needing every new purse they see in a magazine, which, of course, we don't care at all about, we think we need to look like the super "douches" with tons of inheritance money that we see in magazines. It's no different. So forget about that because now you know that women are not attracted to guys with money. They're not attracted to good looks. They're not attracted to huge muscles and they're not attracted to a full head of hair.

What women are really attracted to is "pre-selection". That's it. That's all. Everything else is a lie. But knowing exactly what to mimic to use "pre-selection" to attract flocks of women is everything. You may not know this but the average man sleeps with about seven women in his life and while I'm nothing more than just an average guy, when I started using "pre-selection" to get women to chase me, I was completely broke and still living in my car and I was sleeping with more than 15 new, young, hot women a month.

I was going through an entire life of awesome sex every two weeks. Now, I wasn't born with good looks. I wasn't blessed with horse-sized manhood and I'm not even remotely close to strong or muscular. In fact, I'm short. I weigh about 130 pounds when I'm soaking wet and I suck at sports. And here's the real kicker - I grew up in a trailer park.

But after wasting my whole life believing the lie that women actually cared about that stuff, I finally came across this embarrassingly simple, tested and proven process for making women immediately think that I have a waiting list just to date me.

Whenever I feel like it, I use this technique to get a new chick to come back to my place with little or absolutely no effort at all, without spending a dime doing it or risking rejection in the process. And if I can do it, you can do it.

Here's something I didn't know for most of my life. Every time a woman decides to sleep with a man, she goes through the same four-step process. If you know this simple, four-step process, you can take any woman you want through it without her even knowing and she will become intimate with you within a matter of minutes. It's really out of her control.

It's scary to some people to think that there's a technique that any guy could do that would create attraction in a woman's subconscious.

People wonder a lot - what is it? Is it real? And if it is actually legal? Well, it's technically legal because no one has any proof that you're using it in the first place. But when word got out that I was teaching it to average guys around the world, I started seeing some serious heat from the press anyway. I got a called from NBC to come on The Today Show. I had a top-rated show in current TV revolving around me and my strange but effective techniques. I've been mentioned in dozens of newspapers, online magazines and all that stuff and I landed a top-rated satellite radio show on SiriusXM.

But you have to remember this. I'm just a reformed little "wuss" with women who was just too tired of being walked all over to take it anymore. I wanted to have the women I knew I deserve, just like I'm sure you do.

I didn't want to settle for the ones I knew I could easily get just like you don't want to settle either. My name is Josh Pellicer and I'm the creator of The Tao of Badass. This is another way of saying the way of the badass.

I've heard a lot of guys call it "The Stealth Seduction System" because it's completely under the radar. But it's more like a step-by-step attraction blueprint that shows an average guy exactly what this four-step process is and how to use it.

This is the very first step-by-step guide that uses

a proven method for attracting any woman, even the first time you use it, without changing who you are, memorizing stupid lines or creeping women out. Even if you're over the age of 50 and you want to date younger women, if you're balding, if you're overweight and lazy, you are not rich, and you're definitely afraid of approaching women, and especially if you've tried everything you could think of and you're still not seeing the results you really want.

There is so much hyperbole in the above section of text that it is difficult to know where to begin. So, let's focus on just a few of the claims:

- The only thing women want is "pre-selection" – "That's all", he says. "Everything else is a lie."

- "Pre-selection" works for anybody – even short, scrawny, broke guys living in their car

- If Pellicer can do it, you can do it

- His techniques work on a woman "within minutes", "without her even knowing" and her responses are "really out of her control"

- His "step-by-step guide" will even work for men "over the age of 50" who "want to date younger women", guys who are "overweight and lazy", "not rich", "afraid of approaching women" and - *most important of all* – guys who have "tried everything [they] could think of" and are "still not seeing the results [they] really want"

This last category is, perhaps, the biggest one of all.

Guys who have tried everything and are still not seeing the results they want.

That is the *real* target market for **The Tao of Badass**.

Guys who just can't figure out a way to attract women and are desperate enough to resort to anything – even tricking, duping and deceiving women into sleeping with them.

If you're in *that* category – Pellicer's **Tao of Badass** is your salvation:

There's nothing simpler, easier to use and more effective than the Tao System. Now I've revealed some pretty controversial secrets on this webinar - secrets that frankly I could get into a lot of trouble for revealing.

You now know that looking at a woman's mouth at the right time will make her uncontrollably daydream about sleeping with you. You learned that facing a woman directly when you first meet her will completely and instantly turn her off. You learned that just by saying one sentence, you can make any woman compete for your attention and chase after you, and you found out that women actually don't want money, big muscles or a full head of hair or good looks. You now know – and this is what will get me in a lot of

trouble – that women are actually attracted to "pre-selection" and that you can follow a few simple steps to use "pre-selection" and turn on any woman you want.

I also revealed the secret behind a woman's filter mechanism and that you can bypass it and stay under the radar while you're doing it. Now, you can take this information that I've taught here today and it will work or you can do what many guys do and get a head start by learning the full set of sexual triggers that most men will never know - sexual triggers designed to keep her interested in you, sexual triggers designed to make her become addicted to you, some triggers that will guarantee that she will fall in love with you and some that will make you so confident around hot women, that they will be competing with each other for you the moment they see you.

Each trigger comes with simple step-by-step instructions to make sure you get it right every time. If you're one of those guys that want to learn this stuff over time, then go ahead and close this video now because the next secret I'm going to reveal is only for guys who want my quick start version.

Yeah, you might be a little impatient but you know what you want and you don't want to waste your time with unnecessary trial and error. If that sounds like you, then you're going to want to know about my Ultimate Badass Solution. You cannot find this solution anywhere else, mostly because no one knows the secrets to bypass her logical brain that I do. It's not some complicated 100-step process. It's not a recycled version of something you've heard of before. It's brand new and I'm revealing it right now for the first time.

It has been secretly tested by thousands of guys who are in my inner circle and I'm ready to open up this test to a few new guys who are ready to use these techniques to attract some sexy, young women.

But I'm only interested in revealing my full system to a specific kind of guy. So if you're already really good with women and you don't want to know exactly how to seduce and attract every hot chick you meet, then close this video now and do not continue watching.

I'm not here to make the rich richer and the poor poorer, man. I want to empower guys like me. So if you've ever gone a month or longer without exciting, crazy sex with a new, young, hot woman, if you ever had a girl that you liked stolen by some loud douche, if you feel too old, too ugly, fat, bald, or weak to date the most desirable women on the planet without having to chase them or buy them anything or if you're just tired of having to constantly try to get women interested in you, then I want to download my brain into your head.

Once again, there is a large mass of hot air to wade through here, although much of it is a reiteration of what he said has said earlier – all that palaver about "looking at a women's mouth at the right time" to make her "uncontrollably daydream about sleeping with you", not "facing a woman directly when you first meet her" and "saying one sentence" that can "make any woman compete for your attention and chase after you" – yes, it's all there - just in case you didn't get it the first or the second or the third time.

But what is more significant – and more sinister - than the repetition of the preposterous claims, in my opinion, is the recurring theme of *controlling women*.

The sexual triggers that Pellicer wants to share with you are "designed to keep her interested in you", "make her addicted to you" and will "guarantee that she will fall in love with you".

If you're a guy who has tried everything and you're still not seeing the results you really want, Pellicer has come along to save *your ass* with *his ass* – his **Ultimate Badass Solution**.

How are you supposed to resist *that*?

But wait a minute!

He's only interested in revealing his full system to "a specific kind of guy".

And what kind of guy is that?

A guy who has "gone a month or longer without exciting, crazy sex with a new, young, hot woman", a guy who has had a girl that he liked "stolen by some loud douche", a guy who feels "too old, fat, bald or weak to date the most desirable women on the planet" and finally, a guy who is "just tired of having to constantly try to get women interested in [him]".

That's the "specific kind of guy" that Pellicer is interested in "empowering".

Is there *anything* in that description that sounds like it might apply *to you?*

What about the bit about having "gone a month or longer without exciting, crazy sex with a new, young, hot woman"?

There are a lot of qualifiers in that phrase that could very well land you right in Pellicer's crosshairs, and I'm guessing that one of them is the word "crazy".

If you've gone a month or longer without "crazy" sex – you need **The Tao of Badass**.

Forget the part about new, young and hot.

"Crazy" is what has tripped you up.

And just about every other guy on earth.

In the next chapter, we'll examine the components of Pellicer's **Ultimate Badass Solution**.

CHAPTER 5

The Offer

In the next section of text, Pellicer lets us in on some of the contents of his **Tao System**. Before doing so, however, he offers up social proof in the form of testimonials:

Let me show you something that will really surprise you. This is the Facebook message I got a little while ago.

"Seriously, I was a loser with women a few months ago. Women love me and they want to be with me."

Here's another one, an email: "I truly feel free from my low self-esteem."

As lame as these testimonials are, they reveal a significant pattern. They are from men who have issues with self-esteem – one refers to himself as a "loser" and the other says that he feels free from his "low self-esteem".

This, as we have seen, is the real target market for **The Tao of Badass** – guys who lack confidence with women and are desperate enough to try *anything* – even something as patently ridiculous as **The Tao System**.

Once again, Pellicer issues a call to the "specific kind of guy" he is looking to "empower":

Now, if you're not the most suave guy in the world, if you're nervous or hesitant around women, or if you're not as confident as you used to be or would like to be, then man, I want you to use this and be better with women than you could ever dream of.

Up to this point in the video, we have been given a taste of what the **Tao System** includes in the form of techniques like "propinquity". "consistency" and "pre-selection".

In the next section of the text, Pellicer reveals more - although still, only *a fraction* - of what he promises to deliver in return for your $67.

I will quote the text of in its entirety so as to avoid any claims that I am misrepresenting it:

Let me just tell you about a fraction of what's in the Tao System.

The Self-Fulfilling Prophecy Qualifier. This is an under-the-radar phrase that I say word-for-word that will instantly transform any woman into my private sex slave and compel her to follow me around like a puppy dog without having to even think about competing with other dudes for her attention.

I got an email from Benjamin D. from this. He said, "This technique has been magic. I've realized I much prefer to be chased than the other way around." Yeah, no crap.

The Make-Out Technique. This one I hesitated to share at first because this was my bread and butter for a while but with this technique, I can say one simple and seemingly innocent phrase to any woman and make her lean in for a kiss, even if she wasn't attracted to me in the first place.

Cesar G. sent me an email saying, "Man, does that phrase work!"

Instant Dominance. Now this is something I use when I want a woman to be submissive around me. It's extremely arousing and almost intimidating to women whenever I do it. Do you know what it's like to make a "super hot" girl actually become noticeably turned on right in front of your eyes? It's empowering.

I got an email from Michael saying, "It has completely changed my thoughts and solidified my self-confidence in conversation with women."

The High Value Hello. This is a change in the way I introduce myself to her that will get her aroused before I finish saying hello. On page 114, I reveal 10 undeniable ways that you can know for sure that a woman is attracted to you regardless of what she says because it only takes one missed, "I want you to do me right now," message from her to completely ruin your chances of hooking up.

That brings me to another thing you're going to discover. How to read a woman's eye movements to tell me whether she's lying, telling the truth, a visual thinker, naturally creative, and even if she has a secret and she doesn't want you to know about it.

You will know women better than they know themselves and it's actually going to be easy. It will be embarrassingly obvious to you once you know this simple but weird trick. This eye-reading trick developed originally by the FBI is powerful, proven psychology made simple and applied to work for you and to help you attract women effortlessly.

You will also discover the truth about attractive body language because I'm going to teach you the secret difference between positive body language and dominant body language on page 104. You will learn how you can use it to command attention and attract women at the same time.

Jimmy wrote me an email to tell me that, "Women smile and talk to me more. Men seem to respect me more," when he started using this technique.

You will also discover the truth about a woman's tests. Women give men three secret tests that most men will absolutely fail and when you fail even one of these tests, even if you only screw up one time, you will blow it with the nines and tens and only attract women that are fours and fives.

On page 87, you will discover what to say when a woman asks you to buy her a drink in a way that compels her to buy you a drink and flirt with you.

On page 57, you will learn how to tell early if she's planning on putting you in the friend zone and the one thing you can say to reverse it and make her think of you as a potential boyfriend.

I got an email from James saying, "Learning how to manage the tests that will instantly tell a woman whether to put you in the friend zone or the date zone has been awesome."

Women play loads of mind games with men and we hate it but they have to. Women need to give out tests in order to feel safe. The goal isn't to make her stop playing these games. It's to turn these games on their head. You have to know how to pass them. That's the only way to stay in control, draw women to you and accomplish what 99 percent of men just can't. The only way you can pass them is with the techniques you will learn in the Tao System where I will reveal how you can make it look easy.

What about flirting? Well, you're doing it completely backward if you're doing what the experts suggest you do. I'm going to give you a simple change in your flirting on page 51 that will automatically bypass her logical brain and speak directly to her emotions to make her feel attracted to you.

Really hot women get a lot of other guys staring at them and trying to steal them away but in Tao, I will teach you a simple trick to keep a woman from ever cheating on you, to keep her by your side forever. This technique is super ninja.

Since I found this out, I've done it in every relationship I've been in and it saved my ass on more than one occasion.

Want to know how to read her mind? Well, on page 97, I reveal a weird trick that shows how you can read the content and the context of body language and this is my favorite. To give you a superhuman-like ability to read a woman and know their fears, desires and secrets instantly.

And Tao isn't about fluff or filler. It's filled with easy to understand, proven and cutting-edge knowledge and technology built on what women are really attracted to. It's not complicated or hard to read. I'm not some scientist who's trying to wow you with his huge vocabulary. It's broken down so that regular guys like you and me can understand it.

Aki says, "I love the fact that you broke it down and rationalized it in an easy-to-digest and understandable way."

Now the price? I'm going to get to that in just a few seconds. But I want to tell you something first. If you're interested in a system for making a woman fall in love with you, then first you will have to read the disclaimer on the first page of chapter eight. It reads, "If you would like love to stay magical for you instead of viewing it as a process that you can control, then you should skip this chapter," because in chapter eight, I reveal the step by step process that every woman goes through when she falls deeply in love with a man.

I reveal tools that you can use to make a woman fall in love with you. It's a powerful tool and if you want it, as soon as you pick up Tao, you will want to turn straight to chapter eight to get it.

Fernando posted on our member are, "I use this technique and guess what, she's my girlfriend now."

Ever said something to a woman and as the words are leaving your mouth, you realize it was just the absolute wrong thing to say? Well, on page 39, you will discover a simple thing that you could do to erase that from your natural behavior and of course I reveal the right things to say as well.

Looking for a step by step visual guide to attracting women? Well, by ordering today, only from this page, you will get a do-this-then-do-that flowchart to take you from having never met a girl straight through to getting her laughing, chasing you, and in the mood.

I got an email from Russell S telling me, "I follow

it and it works like a charm." It's called The Map of Interaction Flowchart. If you're a beginner, you're really going to enjoy what you uncover on page 73. It's a comprehensive manual on how to approach women properly to create attraction immediately.

For the more advanced guys, the system outlined on page 45 will up your game like crazy. So what's the price for this brand new secret system? Well, let's face it. Personal consulting in my line of work is not cheap and neither is paying for expensive dinners, drinks, clothes and maintaining monthly fees for online dating sites. I won't even talk about how expensive it can be to undo the negative effects that failing with women can have on your self-esteem.

Plus if you go out and pick up some cheesy "Men Are From Mars" book, you're going to get absolutely nothing in the way of actual, usable techniques and you will be left all alone without any support or help from like-minded guys like yourself.

With Tao, you get ongoing support forever as a member. What do you think a fair price would be? Four hundred and ninety-five dollars would be more than fair considering all the bonus products I'm about to give you. But you're not going to pay $495. You won't pay $295 either. You won't even pay $149. By ordering today only through this webinar, you get the entire Tao of Badass Complete Attraction System plus nine additional complete bonus products I'm about to show you for only $67, fully guaranteed for 60 days.

Try it. See how well it works for you. If for any reason you don't fall in love with the Tao System, simply ask us for a refund and we will give it to you, every penny without questions or hassles. You can keep all the bonus books just for giving it a shot.

Rob posted in the members area, "I was amazed at how well it worked. It's the best investment ever."

Here's an email from Pablo. It says, "I feel like a kid with a new toy and I want to talk about how amazing it is."

David posted in the members area as well, "Since I discovered your program, my social life has improved ten million fold and talking to women has become a natural thought for me."

I even got an email from Jessica S. The chick says, "I'm a woman. Your advice is good, ethical and it works."

I also got a really great email from Craig saying he has gone from having no girlfriend to having more sex than he has ever had in his life. And he says, "P.S. In the time I've been writing this, I've had two text messages from two women."

Now let me introduce you to your nine free bonus products.

- The Dating Multiples Report – This is a complete guide to dating multiple women at the same time and how to have them love you for it, without lying, tricking them, cheating or being a player and a secret hidden way to eliminate jealousy in any relationships.

- The Cheat-Proof Yourself Report – This handy little guide will teach you the secret tool that will make you look like the only guy who exists in the world.

- Escaping the Friend-Zone –If you've ever been trapped in the friend zone, and you wanted to be more than just friends but you didn't know how, you know how much it completely sucks. Well this report will teach you the advanced techniques needed to make sure that never happens and how to get out of it if it does.

- The Guide to Breaking-Up Report – Now as you go on your journey, you will have to end relationships with women that you will care a lot about because at the end of the day, you will probably only be able to choose one. When the time comes, if you don't know the exact steps to do in the right order, you will cause a tornado of pain and suffering to those women. This guide teaches you word for word tips to get you through it and out the other side still being friends.

- The Author's Unabridged Audio Commentary narrated by myself – You want an inside look into my thoughts behind each of the secrets I reveal in Tao? Well this audio commentary will walk you through a new way of approaching these secrets uncensored and straight from the source.

- You will also get this special bonus. Module one of my live ground-breaking Hacking Attraction Course. Along my path to discover the super powers that we can hone and use to have women begging us for sex, I uncovered something absolutely fascinating. There are four major different types of super skills that a guy can have. Now this brand new program reveals those skills and walks you through to find yours and of course once you find it, how to use it effectively to attract the hottest women on the planet.

- Now you also have my Banter Cheat Sheet. I wanted to put an end to the whole "What do I say when I walk up to her?" thing. So I created this cheat sheet for you to access anytime to get new, creative, funny things to say that will build massive amounts of attraction with the women you meet. You will get a lifetime access to the frequently updated Banter Cheat Sheet as a bonus. So on there, you will see word for word, proven "what to say" lines that make women smile and open up to you.

- Finally, your super bonus, the world-renowned five-week Body Language Mastery Course. If you order now, I will throw in my complete Body Language Training Course which is a $1700 value for free. In this five-week intensive program, I reveal the five pillars of sex appeal. You have to jump onboard to check it out and see just what those five pillars are. But once you get into it, you will agree with the rest of my advanced students. The five-week Body Language Mastery Course is the most effective program ever discovered for turning women on without even opening your mouth.

All of this for only $67 fully guaranteed for 60 days. I want you to click on the button below this video that says, "Click to Order Now" because you want to be with more beautiful women and I've got a proven, easy-to-use attraction system for you that is guaranteed to do exactly that.

And if you order now, I will also give you lifetime access to the Tao members-only private community which is a $200 value absolutely free.

If you want to join the thousands of Tao

members that are getting all their questions answered right now, then log in instantly by clicking the orange "Click to Order Now" button below this video.

Once you click the orange "Click to Order Now" button below, you will be taken instantly to a secure checkout page and you will be confident knowing that your data is private and guaranteed secure by McAfee and VeriSign with 128-bit encryption.

And then within a matter of seconds, you will unlock the secrets within the Tao System and have the most desirable women eating out of the palm of your hand tonight.

In marketing parlance, the section of text that is quoted above is referred to as the "offer".

Pellicer begins his offer by itemizing specific components in the **Tao System,** such as "The Self-Fulfilling Prophecy Qualifier", "The Make-out Technique", "Instant Dominance" and "The High-Value Hello".

Interwoven with these components are additional testimonials from buyers, along with references to specific pages of text, such as, "On page 57 you will learn how to tell early if she's planning on putting you in the 'friend zone' and the one thing you can say to reverse it and make her think of you as a potential boyfriend."

All of this is intended – believe it or not – to lend credibility to the offer.

Not surprisingly, the main themes and motifs introduced in earlier sections of the video are back again in full force:

- Exerting control over women – The Self-Fulfilling Prophecy Qualifier, Pellicer says, will transform any woman into his "private sex slave". Another component, actually specifically called "Instant Dominance", is used to make a woman "submissive"

- The reliance upon "simple but weird" tricks, such as the "eye-reading trick developed originally by the F.B.I."

- The obsessive focus on women as sexual objects – as in "really hot women get a lot of other guys staring at them and trying to steal them away"

- Scientific-sounding statements such as, "that's the only way to stay in control, draw women to you and accomplish what 99% of men just can't" and "women need to give out tests in order to feel safe"

- Preposterous claims for the efficacy of the product such as, "I can say one simple and embarrassingly innocent phrase to any woman and make her lean in for a kiss" and "I will teach you a simple trick to keep a woman from ever cheating on you, to keep her by your side forever"

- And, if I may inject a personal note here - my favorite of all of the absurd claims – "The five-week Body Language Mastery Course is the most effective program ever discovered for turning women on without even opening your mouth"

Included in the information about the offer is, of course, the price, which, in the case of **The Tao of Badass** system, is $67.

If you pay that, Pellicer promises, you will have "the most desirable women eating out of the palm of your hand tonight".

I hope that by now you *are* laughing at the sheer audacity of these ridiculous claims – but what you should *not* be laughing at, in my opinion – and what I am *certainly* not laughing at is the toxic message at the sinister heart of **The Tao of Badass** system.

If you were to allow yourself to be infected with the toxic ideas and attitudes about dating, relationships, women and sex presented in the **Tao of Badass** promotional video – and, presumably, in the product itself – you might just do yourself and others a great deal of harm – *in my opinion.*

These toxic ideas and attitudes will not only *not help you attract women into your life*, they will more than likely guarantee that you don't.

In the next chapter, I will explain why.

CHAPTER 6

How to Identify and Reject Toxic Ideas

As I noted in Chapter 1 of this book, **The Tao of Badass** promotional video begins with a warning to viewers that the content of the video may be offensive to some viewers.

This, as it turns out, is the only truthful statement in the entire video, as it certainly *does* make good on its warning about containing offensive material, and I am one of those people who finds it offensive.

And so should you.

Let me explain why this video is so objectionable – and why, if you were to buy into *any* of the ideas and attitudes it presents, I believe you would not only undermine your chances of ever achieving happiness with a member of the opposite sex – but you could get yourself into a lot of trouble, too.

As I stated in the Preface, I do not know for sure whether this video – and the product itself – was intended as a joke or as something to be taken seriously.

It is hard to imagine the latter, but it *is* within the realm of possibility – although, just barely.

If you are young, inexperienced, naïve and impressionable, you might just think that what you are being offered in the promotional video that we have been analyzing in the previous chapters is a *real* method or system for meeting and seducing women.

Again, I do not know how impressionable an adolescent male is these days.

Some young men might watch this video and think that it is "on the level" – and - even worse – actually purchase the **Tao of Badass** product.

Somebody has to be buying it, for it to have a gravity rating over 280 in Clickbank!

However - whether this video was intended as satire or as a serious product – what it is *really* presenting is not a *method* of meeting and seducing women but a *fantasy.*

And what is that fantasy?

What is really at the heart of **The Tao of Badass**?

A toxic, sinister *fantasy* of disarming women's natural defense mechanisms and tricking them into providing sexual gratification to you - which they *would not do* if they were able to exercise their free will.

There is a reason why I did not spend pages and pages analyzing the contents of the offer in the previous chapter.

I didn't have to.

All I needed to do was quote the text in its entirety and allow it to reveal its true colours.

Remember the "Self-Fulfilling Prophecy Qualifier"?

The one that Pellicer says "will instantly transform any woman into [his] private sex slave and compel her to follow [him] around like a puppy dog"?

And now, recall the monster in Ohio who kidnapped three young women and kept them *chained* in the basement for over a decade.

He turned them into this "private sex slaves" too.

I'm not suggesting for a moment that he was influenced by **The Tao of Badass** – either the video or the product as, of course, he wasn't.

But he got the idea that he could restrain young women with chains and transform them into his private sex slaves from *somewhere*.

And that "somewhere" is – at least, in part – a culture which incessantly serves up ideas, attitudes and images of women being dominated, subjugated, demeaned, abused and treated as sexual objects.

The entire **Tao System** is constructed, in my view, on these same kinds of ideas, attitudes and images - and uses them to create its fantasy of controlling, subjugating and essentially, *sexually abusing* women.

What else do you call the process of having sex with a woman against her will?

In one of the more revealing statements in the video, Pellicer announces that "a lot of guys" call **The Tao**

of Badass "The "Stealth Seduction System" because it's "completely under the radar".

So is the so-called "dating drug" which renders women unconscious - and you can go to jail for a long time for using that.

The desire to dominate and control women comes out of feelings of helplessness, weakness, powerlessness and frustration.

Many men experience these feelings.

Pellicer – or, whoever created this product – knows this, and that is why the video repeatedly calls out to these men in the hopes that they *might just be* desperate and frustrated enough to resort to trying to *trick or deceive* women into having sex – and he has the gall to tell them that he wants to "empower" them.

Of course, what he is doing is the exact opposite of *empowering* them.

He is shamelessly *exploiting* them!

Even if only *1* out of every 100 guys who watch the video takes it seriously enough to buy the product because of the promise that it will *empower* him – this report will have been worth writing, if it can serve to reveal the video's toxic message about controlling women and the imperative to reject it.

Women hate controlling men, as well they should.

If you *really* want to empower men who feel

powerless – inspire, motivate and provide tools for them to get the most that they can out of themselves.

Making the most of your talents and abilities is *real* power – and the only form of power we can *really* have.

If you want to overcome feelings of helplessness, you must develop the skills, abilities and talents to help yourself.

Once you do that, you will start attracting women – and lots of other good things too – into your life.

Like everything else of value, the attention of a woman, the love of a woman and yes – *the pleasure of having sex with a woman* – has to be *earned*.

Sorry to be the one to break the bad news to you but - *nobody* likes a loser.

"You can't always get what you want" - to quote the classic Rolling Stones song - and the sooner you learn that lesson, the better off you are going to be – not only in terms of dealing with women, but in life.

But - if you do the work *on yourself* that is required to make the most of the natural gifts that you have been given – again, as the Stones said – "you might just get what you need".

At the heart of **The Tao of Badass** philosophy is the toxic, sinister and infantile *fantasy* that you *can* get what you want – or, to be more specific – that you can have sex anytime you want with "the most attractive women on the planet" - by using tricks, techniques or a "stealth seduction system" to force them to act *against their will*.

Why would an idea as ridiculous as that be true?

If it was intended as a joke – it's not funny.

If it was meant to be taken seriously – it's even worse.

So, if you can't trick, dupe or deceive women into having sex with you - what can you do?

You can start by facing reality – it's really not that bad.

Another thing you can do is to review the passages that I have quoted from the promotional script for **The Tao of Badass** and make note of any words, terms or expressions that are condescending or demeaning to women.

I've pointed out a number of them, but there are many that I haven't drawn your attention to.

Once you've found them in the script, make sure you delete them permanently from your vocabulary - and your brain - as they are offensive to women, and to a lot of men, as well.

Here are a few more suggestions that you might find helpful:

- Understand that seeing women that you find attractive is a constant in a man's life but it doesn't mean that you have to approach every woman you see or that you have some kind of God-given right to *be with* every woman you meet.

- Recognize that women have the right to be attracted to whomever they wish and that the desire to dupe or deceive them into thinking that *you* are someone or something you are not is disrespectful, immature and wrong.

- Be honest and direct in your dealings with women and with everyone else, as well. Don't play "head games" or to try to impress women with any kind of false, inauthentic behaviour. Memorizing "pick-up" lines or clever banter is plain idiotic, so don't do it.

- Understand that there are no magic bullets that will attract women so stop looking for them and accept the fact that, as in every other facet of life, you win some and you lose some. If you really want to be in a relationship and you are a caring, considerate and loving person, you will find someone who is looking for those qualities. If you don't have those qualities, work on developing them. If you want others to be interested in you, begin by being interested in others, and in the many interesting things that are going on in the world. Women are attracted to men they find interesting, so become one of those men.

- Be nice. That's right, nice. Women like nice

guys and why wouldn't they? The next time you see a woman that you think is attractive with a guy who doesn't seem to have a ton of money, big muscles or GQ good looks, don't assume that he used silly techniques or tactics to attract her. Assume, instead, that he's a good guy who treats his girlfriend with respect, enjoys doing nice things for her and cares for her as a person, not just as a sexual object, because that is more than likely the truth.

- Develop an internal "bullshit detector" to filter out creeps, charlatans and con men who try to tell you that women don't like the things that your brain tells you every day that they do – i.e. guys who are attractive, fit, successful, smart, interesting and nice. Why wouldn't they? If you feel that you could stand to improve in any of those areas – do it. It's a tough, competitive world so why should *you* be the one to get something for nothing? You don't have to be perfect and no one is. But you should try to make the most of your talents and abilities because that is the best way to get what you want in life.

- Recognize that sleeping with or even dating more than one woman at a time is selfish and inconsiderate and always leads to trouble so don't do it.

- Be appreciative of the attention of women

and recognize that it is a gift to which you have no entitlement, whatsoever.

And, finally, avoid *anything* purporting to be a system for "seducing women" or "picking up women" as it is virtually guaranteed to contain the same kind of toxic ideas and attitudes that we have been examining in this book.

About the Author

Alan Stransman is a former teacher of English and Film at the high school and university levels, and award-winning television producer/writer/director. Among his many television credits is the series **Spectacular Spas**, which he created, wrote, produced and directed, and which was broadcast in more than 50 countries worldwide.

Alan Stransman also founded one of the first day spas in the world for men, called The Men's PowerSpa in downtown Toronto. He wrote a book about that experience entitled**, Don't Let Your Dream Business Turn Into a Nightmare: A Cautionary Tale for Would-Be Entrepreneurs** www.mybusinessnightmare.com, which was adapted into a case study by the Ivey School of Business at the University of Western Ontario, and taught in entrepreneurship programs at colleges and universities. He also wrote the memoir, "**So, Why Have You Never Been Married?": A Memoir of Love, Loss and Lunacy**, which he describes as " a love letter to the women in my life whom I have loved, lost and never forgotten".

Alan Stransman is the author of several other books, all of which are available on Amazon. He has a Master's degree in English Literature form the University of Western Ontario and a Master's degree in Communications from the Newhouse School of Communications at Syracuse University.

www.ingramcontent.com/pod-product-compliance
Lightning Source LLC
Chambersburg PA
CBHW050558280326
41933CB00011B/1888